Bible Promises

Compiled by
Dr. Terry L. Booher, Pastor
Faith Baptist Church
Fort Pierce, Florida

"He staggered not at the promise of God through unbelief; but was strong in faith, giving glory to God; And being fully persuaded that, what he had promised, he was able also to perform," Romans 4:20,21.

Table of Contents

Anger	47
Backsliding	48
Bible, The	8
Cheer	23
Church, The	57
Comfort	22
Contentment	46
Courage	9
Depression	45
Doubt	34
Elderly	67
Eternal Life	28
Eternity	53
Faith	52
Faithfulness	37
Family	64
Fear	15
Fellowship	62
Financial	50
Forgiveness	18
Giving, Stewardship	58
God's Grace	55
Godliness	38
Heaven	31
Holy Spirit, The	56
Hope	4
Humility	40
Influence	68
Joy	40

Love	6
Loneliness	27
Marriage	63
Obedience	54
Old Age	32
Patience	12
Peace	23, 42
Prayer	21
Prosperity	69
Protection	5
Reaping, Sowing	41
Righteousness	43
Salvation	24
Satan	59
Second Coming, The	60
Security	10
Sickness	26
Sin	33
Single People	66
Strength	44
Sorrow, Grief	49
Submission	48
Temptation	14
Trouble	36
Widows	65
Will of God, The	29
Work	42
Worry	17

Hope

2 Corinthians 5:17, "Therefore if any man be in Christ, he is a new creature: old things are passed away; behold, all things are become new."

Psalm 68:19, "Blessed be the Lord, who daily loadeth us with benefits, even the God of our salvation."

Psalm 86:5, "For thou, Lord, art good, and ready to forgive; and plenteous in mercy unto all them that call upon thee."

Isaiah 50:7, "For the Lord GOD will help me; therefore shall I not be confounded: therefore have I set my face like a flint, and I know that I shall not be ashamed."

John 15:7, "If ye abide in me, and my words abide in you, ye shall ask what ye will, and it shall be done unto you."

John 14:13, "And whatsoever ye shall ask in my name, that will I do, that the Father may be glorified in the Son."

Psalm 37:4, "Delight thyself also in the LORD; and he shall give thee the desires of thine heart."

Psalm 107:9, "For he satisfieth the longing soul, and filleth the hungry soul with goodness."

Joel 2:26, "And ye shall eat in plenty, and be satisfied, and praise the name of the LORD your God, that hath dealt wondrously with you: and my people shall never be ashamed."

John 6:35, "And Jesus said unto them, I am the bread of life: he that cometh to me shall never hunger; and he that believeth on me shall never thirst."

Romans 8:32, "He that spared not his own Son, but delivered him up for us all, how shall he not with him also freely give us all things?"

1 Corinthians 2:9, "But as it is written, Eye hath not seen, nor ear heard, neither have entered into the heart of man, the things which God hath prepared for them that love him."

Joshua 1:8, "This book of the law shall not depart out of thy mouth; but thou shalt meditate therein day and night, that thou mayest observe to do according to all that is written therein: for then thou shalt make thy way prosperous, and then thou shalt have good success."

Isaiah 40:31, "But they that wait upon the LORD shall renew their strength; they shall mount up with wings as eagles; they shall run, and not be weary; and they shall walk, and not faint."

Protection

Psalm 3:3, "But thou, O LORD, art a shield for me; my glory, and the lifter up of mine head."

1 Samuel 2:9, "He will keep the feet of his saints, and the wicked shall be silent in darkness; for by strength shall no man prevail."

Zephania 3:17, "The LORD thy God in the midst of thee is mighty; he will save, he will rejoice over thee with joy; he will rest in his love, he will joy over thee with singing."

Deuteronomy 33:27, "The eternal God is thy refuge, and underneath are the everlasting arms: and he shall thrust out the enemy from before thee; and shall say, Destroy them."

Isaiah 59:19, "So shall they fear the name of the LORD from the west, and his glory from the rising of the sun. When the enemy shall come in like a flood, the Spirit of the LORD shall lift up a standard against him."

2 Thessalonians 3:3, "But the Lord is faithful, who shall stablish you, and keep you from evil."

Psalm 91:7, "A thousand shall fall at thy side, and ten thousand at thy right hand; but it shall not come nigh thee."

Revelation 3:20, "Behold, I stand at the door, and knock: if any man hear my voice, and open the door, I will come in to him, and will sup with him, and he with me."

Hebrews 13:5, "Let your conversation be without covetousness; and be content with such things as ye have: for he hath said, I will never leave thee, nor forsake thee."

2 Thessalonians 3:3, "But the Lord is faithful, who shall stablish you, and keep you from evil."

2 Chronicles 16:9a, "For the eyes of the LORD run to and fro throughout the whole earth, to show himself strong in the behalf of them whose heart is perfect toward him."

Exodus 23:22, "But if thou shalt indeed obey his voice, and do all that I speak; then I will be an enemy unto thine enemies, and an adversary unto thine adversaries."

1 Peter 3:12, "For the eyes of the Lord are over the righteous, and his ears are open unto their prayers: but the face of the Lord is against them that do evil."

Psalm 63:1, "O God, thou art my God; early will I seek thee: my soul thirsteth for thee, my flesh longeth for thee in a dry and thirsty land, where no water is;"

ൟൟ Love ൟൟ
God's Love for Us

Romans 5:8, "But God commendeth his love toward us, in that, while we were yet sinners, Christ died for us."

John 3:16, "For God so loved the world, that he gave his only begotten Son, that whosoever believeth in him should not perish, but have everlasting life."

Hosea 2:19, "And I will betroth thee unto me for ever; yea, I will betroth thee unto me in righteousness, and in judgment, and in lovingkindness, and in mercies."

Ephesians 3:17-19, "That Christ may dwell in your hearts by faith; that ye, being rooted and grounded in love, May be able to comprehend with all saints what is the breadth, and length, and depth, and height; And to know the love of Christ, which passeth knowledge, that ye might be filled with all the fulness of God."

1 John 4:10-12, "Herein is love, not that we loved God, but that he loved us, and sent his Son to be the propitiation for our sins. Beloved, if God so loved us, we ought also to love one another. No man hath seen God at any time. If we love one another, God dwelleth in us, and his love is perfected in us."

Proverbs 8:17, "I love them that love me; and those that seek me early shall find me."

John 14:21, "He that hath my commandments, and keepeth them, he it is that loveth me: and he that loveth me shall be loved of my Father, and I will love him, and will manifest myself to him."

Ephesians 2:4, "But God, who is rich in mercy, for his great love wherewith he loved us,"

Romans 5:8, "But God commendeth his love toward us, in that, while we were yet sinners, Christ died for us."

John 15:10, "If ye keep my commandments, ye shall abide in my love; even as I have kept my Father's commandments, and abide in his love."

1 Corinthians 13:7-8, "Beareth all things, believeth all things, hopeth all things, endureth all things. Charity never faileth: but whether there be prophecies, they shall fail; whether there be tongues, they shall cease; whether there be knowledge, it shall vanish away."

Matthew 19:26, "But Jesus beheld them, and said unto them, With men this is impossible; but with God all things are possible."

Galatians 5:22, "But the fruit of the Spirit is love, joy, peace, longsuffering, gentleness, goodness, faith."

The Bible
God's Word

2 Timothy 3:16, "All scripture is given by inspiration of God, and is profitable for doctrine, for reproof, for correction, for instruction in righteousness:"

Isaiah 55:10, 11, "For as the rain cometh down, and the snow from heaven, and returneth not thither, but watereth the earth, and maketh it bring forth and bud, that it may give seed to the sower, and bread to the eater: So shall my word be that goeth forth out of my mouth: it shall not return unto me void, but it shall accomplish that which I please, and it shall prosper in the thing whereto I sent it."

Proverbs 30:5, "Every word of God is pure: he is a shield unto them that put their trust in him."

Hebrews 4:12, "For the word of God is quick, and powerful, and sharper than any twoedged sword, piercing even to the dividing asunder of soul and spirit, and of the joints and marrow, and is a discerner of the thoughts and intents of the heart."

Mark 13:31, "Heaven and earth shall pass away: but my words shall not pass away."

1 Peter 1:25, "But the word of the Lord endureth for ever. And this is the word which by the gospel is preached unto you."

Psalm 119:87, "They had almost consumed me upon

earth; but I forsook not thy precepts."

Matthew 5:18, "For verily I say unto you, Till heaven and earth pass, one jot or one tittle shall in no wise pass from the law, till all be fulfilled."

❧❧❧ Courage ❧❧❧

2 Thessalonians 3:3, "But the Lord is faithful, who shall stablish you, and keep you from evil."

John 15:16, "Ye have not chosen me, but I have chosen you, and ordained you, that ye should go and bring forth fruit, and that your fruit should remain: that whatsoever ye shall ask of the Father in my name, he may give it you."

Isaiah 54:10, "For the mountains shall depart, and the hills be removed; but my kindness shall not depart from thee, neither shall the covenant of my peace be removed, saith the LORD that hath mercy on thee."

James 4:8, "Draw nigh to God, and he will draw nigh to you. Cleanse your hands, ye sinners; and purify your hearts, ye double minded."

Isaiah 43:2, "When thou passest through the waters, I will be with thee; and through the rivers, they shall not overflow thee: when thou walkest through the fire, thou shalt not be burned; neither shall the flame kindle upon thee."

Deuteronomy 1:30, "The LORD your God which goeth before you, he shall fight for you, according to all that he did for you in Egypt before your eyes;"

Philippians 4:19, "But my God shall supply all your need according to his riches in glory by Christ Jesus."

Philippians 4:13, "I can do all things through Christ which strengtheneth me."

Matthew 5:6, "Blessed are they which do hunger and thirst after righteousness: for they shall be filled."

Philippians 4:19, "But my God shall supply all your need according to his riches in glory by Christ Jesus."

Romans 8:37, "Nay, in all these things we are more than conquerors through him that loved us."

Philippians 1:21, "For to me to live is Christ, and to die is gain."

Psalm 27:1, "The LORD is my light and my salvation; whom shall I fear? the LORD is the strength of my life; of whom shall I be afraid?"

Psalm 27:14, "Wait on the LORD: be of good courage, and he shall strengthen thine heart: wait, I say, on the LORD."

John 14:27, "Peace I leave with you, my peace I give unto you: not as the world giveth, give I unto you. Let not your heart be troubled, neither let it be afraid."

Matthew 6:34, "Take therefore no thought for the morrow: for the morrow shall take thought for the things of itself. Sufficient unto the day is the evil thereof."

Deuteronomy 31:6, "Be strong and of a good courage, fear not, nor be afraid of them: for the LORD thy God, he it is that doth go with thee; he will not fail thee, nor forsake thee."

৵৵৵ Security ৵৵৵

Romans 8:38-39, "For I am persuaded, that neither death, nor life, nor angels, nor principalities, nor powers, nor things present, nor things to come, Nor height, nor depth, nor any other creature, shall be able to separate us from the love of God, which is in Christ Jesus our Lord."

Psalm 27:14, "Wait on the LORD: be of good courage, and

he shall strengthen thine heart: wait, I say, on the LORD."
John 6:37, "All that the Father giveth me shall come to me; and him that cometh to me I will in no wise cast out."

Jude 1:24-25, "Now unto him that is able to keep you from falling, and to present you faultless before the presence of his glory with exceeding joy, To the only wise God our Saviour, be glory and majesty, dominion and power, both now and for ever. Amen."

Psalm 23:6, "Surely goodness and mercy shall follow me all the days of my life: and I will dwell in the house of the LORD for ever."

John 6:27, "Labour not for the meat which perisheth, but for that meat which endureth unto everlasting life, which the Son of man shall give unto you: for him hath God the Father sealed."

Isaiah 41:10, "Fear thou not; for I am with thee: be not dismayed; for I am thy God: I will strengthen thee; yea, I will help thee; yea, I will uphold thee with the right hand of my righteousness."

Psalm 31:24, "Be of good courage, and he shall strengthen your heart, all ye that hope in the LORD."

John 10:27-29, "My sheep hear my voice, and I know them, and they follow me: And I give unto them eternal life; and they shall never perish, neither shall any man pluck them out of my hand. My Father, which gave them me, is greater than all; and no man is able to pluck them out of my Father's hand."

1 Peter 1:3-5, "Blessed be the God and Father of our Lord Jesus Christ, which according to his abundant mercy hath begotten us again unto a lively hope by the resurrection of Jesus Christ from the dead, To an inheritance incorruptible, and undefiled, and that fadeth not away, reserved in heaven for you, Who are kept by the power of God through faith unto salvation ready to be revealed in the last time."

Philippians 1:6, "Being confident of this very thing, that he which hath begun a good work in you will perform it until the day of Jesus Christ:"

2 Thessalonians 3:3, "But the Lord is faithful, who shall stablish you, and keep you from evil."

John 6:37, "All that the Father giveth me shall come to me; and him that cometh to me I will in no wise cast out."

Ephesians 4:30, "And grieve not the holy Spirit of God, whereby ye are sealed unto the day of redemption."

Proverbs 30:5, "Every word of God is pure: he is a shield unto them that put their trust in him."

John 14:2-3, "In my Father's house are many mansions: if it were not so, I would have told you. I go to prepare a place for you. And if I go and prepare a place for you, I will come again, and receive you unto myself; that where I am, there ye may be also."

Psalm 37:23, "The steps of a good man are ordered by the LORD: and he delighteth in his way."

Romans 8:31, "What shall we then say to these things? If God be for us, who can be against us?"
Isaiah 40:29, "He giveth power to the faint; and to them that have no might he increaseth strength."

2 Timothy 2:13, "If we believe not, yet he abideth faithful: he cannot deny himself."

Patience

Galations 5:22, "But the fruit of the Spirit is love, joy, peace, longsuffering, gentleness, goodness, faith,"

Hebrews 6:12, "That ye be not slothful, but followers of them who through faith and patience inherit the promises."

Ecclesiastes 7:8-9, "Better is the end of a thing than the beginning thereof: and the patient in spirit is better than the proud in spirit. Be not hasty in thy spirit to be angry: for anger resteth in the bosom of fools."

Psalm 37:8-9, "Cease from anger, and forsake wrath: fret not thyself in any wise to do evil. For evildoers shall be cut off: but those that wait upon the LORD, they shall inherit the earth."

Isaiah 40:1, "Comfort ye, comfort ye my people, saith your God."

Romans 5:3-5, "And not only so, but we glory in tribulations also: knowing that tribulation worketh patience; And patience, experience; and experience, hope: And hope maketh not ashamed; because the love of God is shed abroad in our hearts by the Holy Ghost which is given unto us."

James 5:7-8, "Be patient therefore, brethren, unto the coming of the Lord. Behold, the husbandman waiteth for the precious fruit of the earth, and hath long patience for it, until he receive the early and latter rain. Be ye also patient; stablish your hearts: for the coming of the Lord draweth nigh."

Psalm 37:34, "Wait on the LORD, and keep his way, and he shall exalt thee to inherit the land: when the wicked are cut off, thou shalt see it."

1 Peter 4:12-13, "Beloved, think it not strange concerning the fiery trial which is to try you, as though some strange thing happened unto you: But rejoice, inasmuch as ye are partakers of Christ's sufferings; that, when his glory shall be revealed, ye may be glad also with exceeding joy."

Jeremiah 31:14b, "My people shall be satisfied with my goodness, saith the LORD."

Psalm 107:9, "For he satisfieth the longing soul, and filleth the hungry soul with goodness."

Isaiah 40:31, "But they that wait upon the LORD shall renew their strength; they shall mount up with wings as eagles; they shall run, and not be weary; and they shall walk, and not faint."

James 1:3-5, "Knowing this, that the trying of your faith worketh patience. But let patience have her perfect work, that ye may be perfect and entire, wanting nothing. If any of you lack wisdom, let him ask of God, that giveth to all men liberally, and upbraideth not; and it shall be given him."

Psalm 27:14, "Wait on the LORD: be of good courage, and he shall strengthen thine heart: wait, I say, on the LORD."

Hebrews 10:35-37, "Cast not away therefore your confidence, which hath great recompense of reward. For ye have need of patience, that, after ye have done the will of God, ye might receive the promise. For yet a little while, and he that shall come will come, and will not tarry."

Psalm 33:20, "Our soul waiteth for the LORD: he is our help and our shield."

Hebrews 10:23, "Let us hold fast the profession of our faith without wavering; (for he is faithful that promised;)"

Isaiah 25:9, "And it shall be said in that day, Lo, this is our God; we have waited for him, and he will save us: this is the LORD; we have waited for him, we will be glad and rejoice in his salvation."

❧❧❧ Temptation ❧❧❧

Hebrews 4:16, "Let us therefore come boldly unto the throne of grace, that we may obtain mercy, and find grace to help in time of need."

Romans 6:14, "For sin shall not have dominion over you: for ye are not under the law, but under grace."

Proverbs 28:13, "He that covereth his sins shall not prosper: but whoso confesseth and forsaketh them shall have mercy."

1 Corinthians 10:12-13, "Wherefore let him that thinketh he standeth take heed lest he fall. There hath no temptation taken you but such as is common to man: but God is faithful, who will not suffer you to be tempted above that ye are able; but will with the temptation also make a way to escape, that ye may be able to bear it."

Hebrews 2:18, "For in that he himself hath suffered being tempted, he is able to succour them that are tempted."

2 Peter 2:9a, "The Lord knoweth how to deliver the godly out of temptations,"

James 4:7, "Submit yourselves therefore to God. Resist the devil, and he will flee from you."

1 John 4:4, "Ye are of God, little children, and have overcome them: because greater is he that is in you, than he that is in the world."

James 1:2, 3, 12, "My brethren, count it all joy when ye fall into divers temptations; Knowing this, that the trying of your faith worketh patience. Blessed is the man that endureth temptation: for when he is tried, he shall receive the crown of life, which the Lord hath promised to them that love him."

fear

1 John 4:18, "There is no fear in love; but perfect love casteth out fear: because fear hath torment. He that feareth is not made perfect in love."

Psalm 91:10, "There shall no evil befall thee, neither shall any plague come nigh thy dwelling."

Proverbs 3:25-26, "Be not afraid of sudden fear, neither of the desolation of the wicked, when it cometh. For the LORD shall be thy confidence, and shall keep thy foot from being taken."

Isaiah 54:14, "In righteousness shalt thou be established: thou shalt be far from oppression; for thou shalt not fear: and from terror; for it shall not come near thee."

Psalm 23:4-5, "Yea, though I walk through the valley of the shadow of death, I will fear no evil: for thou art with me; thy rod and thy staff they comfort me. Thou preparest a table before me in the presence of mine enemies: thou anointest my head with oil; my cup runneth over."

Psalm 31:24, "Be of good courage, and he shall strengthen your heart, all ye that hope in the LORD."

Psalm 91:11, "For he shall give his angels charge over thee, to keep thee in all thy ways."

Isaiah 54:14, "In righteousness shalt thou be established: thou shalt be far from oppression; for thou shalt not fear: and from terror; for it shall not come near thee."

Romans 8:2, "For the law of the Spirit of life in Christ Jesus hath made me free from the law of sin and death."

John 8:32, 36, "And ye shall know the truth, and the truth shall make you free. . . If the Son therefore shall make you free, ye shall be free indeed."

2 Corinthians 3:17, "Now the Lord is that Spirit: and where the Spirit of the Lord is, there is liberty."

1 John 4:4, "Ye are of God, little children, and have overcome them: because greater is he that is in you, than he that is in the world."

Psalm 91:1-2, "He that dwelleth in the secret place of the most High shall abide under the shadow of the Almighty. I will say of the LORD, He is my refuge and my fortress: my God; in him will I trust."

1 Peter 5:6, 7, "Humble yourselves therefore under the

mighty hand of God, that he may exalt you in due time: Casting all your care upon him; for he careth for you."

Nehemiah 8:10, "Then he said unto them, Go your way, eat the fat, and drink the sweet, and send portions unto them for whom nothing is prepared: for this day is holy unto our Lord: neither be ye sorry; for the joy of the LORD is your strength."

Psalm 37:3, "Trust in the LORD, and do good; so shalt thou dwell in the land, and verily thou shalt be fed."

2 Timothy 1:7, "For God hath not given us the spirit of fear; but of power, and of love, and of a sound mind."

Psalm 55:22, "Cast thy burden upon the LORD, and he shall sustain thee: he shall never suffer the righteous to be moved."

Isaiah 40:29, "He giveth power to the faint; and to them that have no might he increaseth strength."

Joshua 1:9, "Have not I commanded thee? Be strong and of a good courage; be not afraid, neither be thou dismayed: for the LORD thy God is with thee whithersoever thou goest."

෴෴ Worry ෴෴

Philippians 4:6-7, "Be careful for nothing; but in every thing by prayer and supplication with thanksgiving let your requests be made known unto God. And the peace of God, which passeth all understanding, shall keep your hearts and minds through Christ Jesus."

Isaiah 26:3, "Thou wilt keep him in perfect peace, whose mind is stayed on thee: because he trusteth in thee."

Philippians 4:19, "But my God shall supply all your need according to his riches in glory by Christ Jesus."

Matthew 6:33, "But seek ye first the kingdom of God, and his righteousness; and all these things shall be added unto you."

Romans 8:6, "For to be carnally minded is death; but to be spiritually minded is life and peace."

Hebrews 4:3, "For we which have believed do enter into rest, as he said, As I have sworn in my wrath, if they shall enter into my rest: although the works were finished from the foundation of the world."

Hebrews 4:9, "There remaineth therefore a rest to the people of God."

Psalm 119:165, "Great peace have they which love thy law: and nothing shall offend them."

John 14:27, "Peace I leave with you, my peace I give unto you: not as the world giveth, give I unto you. Let not your heart be troubled, neither let it be afraid."

Forgiveness

Ephesians 1:6-7, "To the praise of the glory of his grace, wherein he hath made us accepted in the beloved. In whom we have redemption through his blood, the forgiveness of sins, according to the riches of his grace;"

2 Corinthians 5:17, "Therefore if any man be in Christ, he is a new creature: old things are passed away; behold, all things are become new."

Psalm 103:12, "As far as the east is from the west, so far hath he removed our transgressions from us."

1 John 2:1, "My little children, these things write I unto you, that ye sin not. And if any man sin, we have an advocate with the Father, Jesus Christ the righteous:"

Colossians 3:13, "Forbearing one another, and forgiving one another, if any man have a quarrel against any: even as Christ forgave you, so also do ye."

Psalm 32:1-2, "A Psalm of David, Maschil. Blessed is he whose transgression is forgiven, whose sin is covered. Blessed is the man unto whom the LORD imputeth not iniquity, and in whose spirit there is no guile."

Isaiah 1:18, "Come now, and let us reason together, saith the LORD: though your sins be as scarlet, they shall be as white as snow; though they be red like crimson, they shall be as wool."

Jeremiah 33:8, "And I will cleanse them from all their iniquity, whereby they have sinned against me; and I will pardon all their iniquities, whereby they have sinned, and whereby they have transgressed against me."

Romans 8:11, "But if the Spirit of him that raised up Jesus from the dead dwell in you, he that raised up Christ from the dead shall also quicken your mortal bodies by his Spirit that dwelleth in you."

John 3:17-18, "For God sent not his Son into the world to condemn the world; but that the world through him might be saved. He that believeth on him is not condemned: but he that believeth not is condemned already, because he hath not believed in the name of the only begotten Son of God."

Psalm 32:1, "Blessed is he whose transgression is forgiven, whose sin is covered."

John 8:10-11, "When Jesus had lifted up himself, and saw none but the woman, he said unto her, Woman, where are those thine accusers? hath no man condemned thee? She said, No man, Lord. And Jesus said unto her, Neither do I condemn thee: go, and sin no more."

Hebrews 10:22, "Let us draw near with a true heart in full assurance of faith, having our hearts sprinkled from an evil conscience, and our bodies washed with pure water."

1 John 1:9, "If we confess our sins, he is faithful and just to forgive us our sins, and to cleanse us from all unrighteousness."

Psalm 103:12, "As far as the east is from the west, so far hath he removed our transgressions from us."

1 John 2:1, "My little children, these things write I unto you, that ye sin not. And if any man sin, we have an advocate with the Father, Jesus Christ the righteous:"

Hebrews 8:12, "For I will be merciful to their unrighteousness, and their sins and their iniquities will I remember no more."
Isaiah 43:25, "I, even I, am he that blotteth out thy transgressions for mine own sake, and will not remember thy sins."

John 5:24, "Verily, verily, I say unto you, He that heareth my word, and believeth on him that sent me, hath everlasting life, and shall not come into condemnation; but is passed from death unto life."

Isaiah 55:7, "Let the wicked forsake his way, and the unrighteous man his thoughts: and let him return unto the LORD, and he will have mercy upon him; and to our God, for he will abundantly pardon."

Mark 11:25, "And when ye stand praying, forgive, if ye have ought against any: that your Father also which is in heaven may forgive you your trespasses."

Matthew 6:1, "Take heed that ye do not your alms before men, to be seen of them: otherwise ye have no reward of your Father which is in heaven."

Matthew 6:14-15, "For if ye forgive men their trespasses, your heavenly Father will also forgive you: But if ye forgive not men their trespasses, neither will your Father forgive your trespasses."

Isaiah 43:18-19, "Remember ye not the former things, neither consider the things of old. Behold, I will do a new thing; now it shall spring forth; shall ye not know it? I will even make a way in the wilderness, and rivers in the desert."

Prayer

Isaiah 65:24, "And it shall come to pass, that before they call, I will answer; and while they are yet speaking, I will hear."

Matthew 7:7-8, "Ask, and it shall be given you; seek, and ye shall find; knock, and it shall be opened unto you: For every one that asketh receiveth; and he that seeketh findeth; and to him that knocketh it shall be opened."

Matthew 18:19-20, "Again I say unto you, That if two of you shall agree on earth as touching any thing that they shall ask, it shall be done for them of my Father which is in heaven. For where two or three are gathered together in my name, there am I in the midst of them."

Mark 11:24, "Therefore I say unto you, What things soever ye desire, when ye pray, believe that ye receive them, and ye shall have them."

John 15:7, "If ye abide in me, and my words abide in you, ye shall ask what ye will, and it shall be done unto you."

Hebrews 4:16, "Let us therefore come boldly unto the throne of grace, that we may obtain mercy, and find grace to help in time of need."

Psalm 37:4, "Delight thyself also in the LORD; and he shall give thee the desires of thine heart."

Psalm 91:15, "He shall call upon me, and I will answer him: I will be with him in trouble; I will deliver him, and honour him."

Psalm 145:18-19, "The LORD is nigh unto all them that call upon him, to all that call upon him in truth. He will fulfil the desire of them that fear him: he also will hear their cry, and will save them."

Proverbs 15:29, "The LORD is far from the wicked: but he heareth the prayer of the righteous."

Matthew 6:6, "But thou, when thou prayest, enter into thy closet, and when thou hast shut thy door, pray to thy Father which is in secret; and thy Father which seeth in secret shall reward thee openly."

Matthew 21:22, "And all things, whatsoever ye shall ask in prayer, believing, ye shall receive."

John 14:13, "And whatsoever ye shall ask in my name, that will I do, that the Father may be glorified in the Son."

John 16:23-24, "And in that day ye shall ask me nothing. Verily, verily, I say unto you, Whatsoever ye shall ask the Father in my name, he will give it you. Hitherto have ye asked nothing in my name: ask, and ye shall receive, that your joy may be full."

Psalm 66:18, "If I regard iniquity in my heart, the Lord will not hear me:"

Psalm 55:17, "Evening, and morning, and at noon, will I pray, and cry aloud: and he shall hear my voice."

ಊಲೋ Comfort, Cheer, Peace ಊಲೋ

1 Peter 1:3-5, "Blessed be the God and Father of our Lord Jesus Christ, which according to his abundant mercy hath begotten us again unto a lively hope by the resurrection of Jesus Christ from the dead, To an inheritance incorruptible, and undefiled, and that fadeth not away, reserved in heaven for you, Who are kept by the power of God through faith unto salvation ready to be revealed in the last time."

Psalm 23:6, "Surely goodness and mercy shall follow me all the days of my life: and I will dwell in the house of the LORD for ever."

Proverbs 8:17, "I love them that love me; and those that seek me early shall find me."

John 14:21, "He that hath my commandments, and keepeth them, he it is that loveth me: and he that loveth me shall be loved of my Father, and I will love him, and will manifest myself to him."

Isaiah 26:3, "Thou wilt keep him in perfect peace, whose mind is stayed on thee: because he trusteth in thee."

Isaiah 9:6, "For unto us a child is born, unto us a son is given: and the government shall be upon his shoulder: and his name shall be called Wonderful, Counsellor, The mighty God, The everlasting Father, The Prince of Peace."

Isaiah 26:12, "LORD, thou wilt ordain peace for us: for thou also hast wrought all our works in us."

Philippians 4:9, "Those things, which ye have both learned, and received, and heard, and seen in me, do: and the God of peace shall be with you."

Psalm 29:11, "The LORD will give strength unto his people; the LORD will bless his people with peace."

John 14:27, "Peace I leave with you, my peace I give unto you: not as the world giveth, give I unto you. Let not your heart be troubled, neither let it be afraid."

Philippians 4:6-7, "Be careful for nothing; but in every thing by prayer and supplication with thanksgiving let your requests be made known unto God. And the peace of God, which passeth all understanding, shall keep your hearts and minds through Christ Jesus."

John 14:23, "Jesus answered and said unto him, If a man love me, he will keep my words: and my Father will love him, and we will come unto him, and make our abode with him."

Psalm 27:10, "When my father and my mother forsake me, then the LORD will take me up."

John 14:18, "I will not leave you comfortless: I will come to you."

1 John 3:2, "Beloved, now are we the sons of God, and it doth not yet appear what we shall be: but we know that, when he shall appear, we shall be like him; for we shall see him as he is."

Philippians 4:6, "Be careful for nothing; but in every thing by prayer and supplication with thanksgiving let your requests be made known unto God."

Galatians 6:9, "And let us not be weary in well doing: for in due season we shall reap, if we faint not."

Psalm 31:24, "Be of good courage, and he shall strengthen your heart, all ye that hope in the LORD."

John 14:18, "I will not leave you comfortless: I will come to you."

Psalm 127:2, "It is vain for you to rise up early, to sit up late, to eat the bread of sorrows: for so he giveth his beloved sleep."

ଈଓଓ Salvation ଈଓଓ

John 6:47, "Verily, verily, I say unto you, He that believeth on me hath everlasting life."

Romans 6:23, "For the wages of sin is death; but the gift of God is eternal life through Jesus Christ our Lord."

2 Corinthians 5:17, "Therefore if any man be in Christ, he is a new creature: old things are passed away; behold, all things are become new."

John 3:36, "He that believeth on the Son hath everlasting life: and he that believeth not the Son shall not see life; but the wrath of God abideth on him."

Revelation 3:20, "Behold, I stand at the door, and knock: if any man hear my voice, and open the door, I will come in to him, and will sup with him, and he with me."
Matthew 10:32, "Whosoever therefore shall confess me before men, him will I confess also before my Father which is in heaven."

1 John 5:11-13, "And this is the record, that God hath given to us eternal life, and this life is in his Son. He that hath the Son hath life; and he that hath not the Son of God hath not life. These things have I written unto you that believe on the name of the Son of God; that ye may know that ye have eternal life, and that ye may believe on the name of the Son of God."

John 20:27-29, "Then saith he to Thomas, Reach hither thy finger, and behold my hands; and reach hither thy hand, and thrust it into my side: and be not faithless, but believing. And Thomas answered and said unto him, My Lord and my God. Jesus saith unto him, Thomas, because thou hast seen me, thou hast believed: blessed are they that have not seen, and yet have believed."

John 6:37, "All that the Father giveth me shall come to me; and him that cometh to me I will in no wise cast out."

1 John 4:14, "And we have seen and do testify that the Father sent the Son to be the Saviour of the world."

Luke 19:10, "For the Son of man is come to seek and to save that which was lost."

John 3:16, "For God so loved the world, that he gave his only begotten Son, that whosoever believeth in him should not perish, but have everlasting life."

Ephesians 2:8-9, "For by grace are ye saved through faith; and that not of yourselves: it is the gift of God: Not of works, lest any man should boast."

Romans 10:9, "That if thou shalt confess with thy mouth the Lord Jesus, and shalt believe in thine heart that God hath raised him from the dead, thou shalt be saved."

John 1:12, "But as many as received him, to them gave he power to become the sons of God, even to them that believe on his name:"

৯৫৯১ Sickness ৯৫৯১

Psa 103:3a, "Who forgiveth all thine iniquities; who healeth all thy diseases;"

Jeremiah 30:17a, "For I will restore health unto thee, and I will heal thee of thy wounds, saith the LORD;"

Exodus 15:26, "And said, If thou wilt diligently hearken to the voice of the LORD thy God, and wilt do that which is right in his sight, and wilt give ear to his commandments, and keep all his statutes, I will put none of these diseases upon thee, which I have brought upon the Egyptians: for I am the LORD that healeth thee."

Jeremiah 17:14, "Heal me, O LORD, and I shall be healed; save me, and I shall be saved: for thou art my praise."

1 Peter 2:24, "Who his own self bare our sins in his own body on the tree, that we, being dead to sins, should live unto righteousness: by whose stripes ye were healed."

Isaiah 53:5, "But he was wounded for our transgressions, he was bruised for our iniquities: the chastisement of our peace was upon him; and with his stripes we are healed."

Proverbs 4:20-22, "My son, attend to my words; incline thine ear unto my sayings. Let them not depart from thine eyes; keep them in the midst of thine heart. For they are life unto those that find them, and health to all their flesh."

James 5:14-15, "Is any sick among you? let him call for the elders of the church; and let them pray over him, anointing him with oil in the name of the Lord: And the prayer of faith shall save the sick, and the Lord shall raise him up; and if he have committed sins, they shall be forgiven him."

Loneliness

Hebrews 13:5, "Let your conversation be without covetousness; and be content with such things as ye have: for he hath said, I will never leave thee, nor forsake thee."

1 Samuel 12:22, "For the LORD will not forsake his people for his great name's sake: because it hath pleased the LORD to make you his people."

Isaiah 41:10, "Fear thou not; for I am with thee: be not dismayed; for I am thy God: I will strengthen thee; yea, I will help thee; yea, I will uphold thee with the right hand of my righteousness."

John 14:18, "I will not leave you comfortless: I will come to you."

John 14:1, "Let not your heart be troubled: ye believe in God, believe also in me."

Psalm 147:3, "He healeth the broken in heart, and bindeth up their wounds."

Romans 8:35-39, "Who shall separate us from the love of Christ? shall tribulation, or distress, or persecution, or famine, or nakedness, or peril, or sword? As it is written, For thy sake we are killed all the day long; we are accounted as sheep for the slaughter. Nay, in all these things we are more than conquerors through him that loved us. For I am persuaded, that neither death, nor life, nor angels, nor principalities, nor powers, nor things present, nor things to come, Nor height, nor depth, nor any other creature, shall be able to separate us from the love of God, which is in Christ Jesus our Lord."

Psalm 46:1, "To the chief Musician for the sons of Korah, A Song upon Alamoth. God is our refuge and strength, a very present help in trouble."

Psalm 27:1, "The LORD is my light and my salvation; whom shall I fear? the LORD is the strength of my life; of whom shall I be afraid?"

Psalm 94:14, "For the LORD will not cast off his people, neither will he forsake his inheritance."

Matthew 28:20, "Teaching them to observe all things whatsoever I have commanded you: and, lo, I am with you alway, even unto the end of the world. Amen."

1 Peter 5:7, "Casting all your care upon him; for he careth for you."

Isaiah 41:17, "When the poor and needy seek water, and there is none, and their tongue faileth for thirst, I the LORD will hear them, I the God of Israel will not forsake them."

Psalm 91:14-15, "Because he hath set his love upon me, therefore will I deliver him: I will set him on high, because he hath known my name. He shall call upon me, and I will answer him: I will be with him in trouble; I will deliver him, and honour him."

Deuteronomy 31:6, "Be strong and of a good courage, fear not, nor be afraid of them: for the LORD thy God, he it is that doth go with thee; he will not fail thee, nor forsake thee."

❧❧❧ Eternal Life ❧❧❧

John 6:47, "Verily, verily, I say unto you, He that believeth on me hath everlasting life."

1 John 5:11, "And this is the record, that God hath given to us eternal life, and this life is in his Son."

John 5:24, "Verily, verily, I say unto you, He that heareth my word, and believeth on him that sent me, hath everlasting life, and shall not come into condemnation; but is passed from death unto life."

John 6:51, "I am the living bread which came down from heaven: if any man eat of this bread, he shall live for ever: and the bread that I will give is my flesh, which I will give for the life of the world."

Psalm 37:18, "The LORD knoweth the days of the upright: and their inheritance shall be for ever."

Psalm 49:15, "But God will redeem my soul from the power of the grave: for he shall receive me."

John 11:25-26, "Jesus said unto her, I am the resurrection, and the life: he that believeth in me, though he were dead, yet shall he live: And whosoever liveth and believeth in me shall never die. Believest thou this?"

John 10:27-28, "My sheep hear my voice, and I know them, and they follow me: And I give unto them eternal life; and they shall never perish, neither shall any man pluck them out of my hand."

John 4:14, "But whosoever drinketh of the water that I shall give him shall never thirst; but the water that I shall give him shall be in him a well of water springing up into everlasting life."

The Will of God

Isaiah 48:17, "Thus saith the LORD, thy Redeemer, the Holy One of Israel; I am the LORD thy God which teacheth thee to profit, which leadeth thee by the way that thou shouldest go."

Isaiah 58:11, "And the LORD shall guide thee continually, and satisfy thy soul in drought, and make fat thy bones: and thou shalt be like a watered garden, and like a spring of water, whose waters fail not."

Psalm 32:8, "I will instruct thee and teach thee in the way which thou shalt go: I will guide thee with mine eye."

Proverbs 6:22-23, "When thou goest, it shall lead thee; when thou sleepest, it shall keep thee; and when thou awakest, it shall talk with thee. For the commandment is a lamp; and the law is light; and reproofs of instruction are the way of life:"

Isaiah 30:21, "And thine ears shall hear a word behind thee, saying, This is the way, walk ye in it, when ye turn to the right hand, and when ye turn to the left."

Psalm 48:14, "For this God is our God for ever and ever: he will be our guide even unto death."

Proverbs 16:3, "Commit thy works unto the LORD, and thy thoughts shall be established."

Psalm 37:23, "The steps of a good man are ordered by the LORD: and he delighteth in his way."

James 1:5, "If any of you lack wisdom, let him ask of God, that giveth to all men liberally, and upbraideth not; and it shall be given him."

Psalm 32:5, "I acknowledged my sin unto thee, and mine iniquity have I not hid. I said, I will confess my transgressions unto the LORD; and thou forgavest the iniquity of my sin."

Joshua 1:8, "This book of the law shall not depart out of thy mouth; but thou shalt meditate therein day and night, that thou mayest observe to do according to all that is written therein: for then thou shalt make thy way prosperous, and then thou shalt have good success."

Psalm 48:14, "For this God is our God for ever and ever: he will be our guide even unto death."

Proverbs 16:3, "Commit thy works unto the LORD, and thy thoughts shall be established."

Proverbs 3:5-6, "Trust in the LORD with all thine heart; and lean not unto thine own understanding. In all thy ways acknowledge him, and he shall direct thy paths."

John 16:13, "Howbeit when he, the Spirit of truth, is come, he will guide you into all truth: for he shall not speak of himself; but whatsoever he shall hear, that shall he speak: and he will show you things to come."

൙൞ Heaven ൙൞

John 14:2-3, "In my Father's house are many mansions: if it were not so, I would have told you. I go to prepare a place for you. And if I go and prepare a place for you, I will come again, and receive you unto myself; that where I am, there ye may be also."

Hebrews 11:16, "But now they desire a better country, that is, an heavenly: wherefore God is not ashamed to be called their God: for he hath prepared for them a city."

Matthew 25:34, "Then shall the King say unto them on his right hand, Come, ye blessed of my Father, inherit the kingdom prepared for you from the foundation of the world:"

1 Corinthians 2:9, "But as it is written, Eye hath not seen, nor ear heard, neither have entered into the heart of man, the things which God hath prepared for them that love him."

1 Thessalonians 4:16-18, "For the Lord himself shall descend from heaven with a shout, with the voice of the archangel, and with the trump of God: and the dead in Christ shall rise first: Then we which are alive and remain shall be caught up together with them in the clouds, to meet the Lord in the air: and so shall we ever be with the Lord. Wherefore comfort one another with these words."

Old Age

Psalm 92:14, "They shall still bring forth fruit in old age; they shall be fat and flourishing;"

Proverbs 3:2, "For length of days, and long life, and peace, shall they add to thee."

Hebrews 13:5, "Let your conversation be without covetousness; and be content with such things as ye have: for he hath said, I will never leave thee, nor forsake thee."

Psalm 23:4, "Yea, though I walk through the valley of the shadow of death, I will fear no evil: for thou art with me; thy rod and thy staff they comfort me."

Romans 8:38-39, "For I am persuaded, that neither death, nor life, nor angels, nor principalities, nor powers, nor things present, nor things to come, Nor height, nor depth, nor any other creature, shall be able to separate us from the love of God, which is in Christ Jesus our Lord."

Psalm 23:6, "Surely goodness and mercy shall follow me all the days of my life: and I will dwell in the house of the **LORD** for ever."

Acts 2:17, "And it shall come to pass in the last days, saith God, I will pour out of my Spirit upon all flesh: and your sons and your daughters shall prophesy, and your young men shall see visions, and your old men shall dream dreams:"

Proverbs 16:31, "The hoary head is a crown of glory, if it be found in the way of righteousness."

Proverbs 22:6, "Train up a child in the way he should go: and when he is old, he will not depart from it."

Proverbs 17:6, "Children's children are the crown of old men; and the glory of children are their fathers."

Sin

Romans 6:23, "For the wages of sin is death; but the gift of God is eternal life through Jesus Christ our Lord."

Romans 5:8, "But God commendeth his love toward us, in that, while we were yet sinners, Christ died for us."

Psalm 32:1, "Blessed is he whose transgression is forgiven, whose sin is covered."

John 8:10-11, "When Jesus had lifted up himself, and saw none but the woman, he said unto her, Woman, where are those thine accusers? hath no man condemned thee? She said, No man, Lord. And Jesus said unto her, Neither do I condemn thee: go, and sin no more."

2 Peter 3:9, "The Lord is not slack concerning his promise, as some men count slackness; but is longsuffering to usward, not willing that any should perish, but that all should come to repentance."

Luke 19:10, "For the Son of man is come to seek and to save that which was lost."

John 3:16, "For God so loved the world, that he gave his only begotten Son, that whosoever believeth in him should not perish, but have everlasting life."

Acts 16:32, "And they spake unto him the word of the Lord, and to all that were in his house."

2 Chronicles 30:9, "For if ye turn again unto the LORD, your brethren and your children shall find compassion before them that lead them captive, so that they shall come again into this land: for the LORD your God is gracious and merciful, and will not turn away his face from you, if ye return unto him."

1 John 1:9, "If we confess our sins, he is faithful and just to forgive us our sins, and to cleanse us from all unrighteousness."

Romans 8:1, "There is therefore now no condemnation to them which are in Christ Jesus, who walk not after the flesh, but after the Spirit."

John 3:18, "He that believeth on him is not condemned: but he that believeth not is condemned already, because he hath not believed in the name of the only begotten Son of God."

Isaiah 55:7, "Let the wicked forsake his way, and the unrighteous man his thoughts: and let him return unto the LORD, and he will have mercy upon him; and to our God, for he will abundantly pardon."

Psalm 11:5, "The LORD trieth the righteous: but the wicked and him that loveth violence his soul hateth."

Doubt

Isaiah 46:10b-11b, "Declaring the end from the beginning, and from ancient times the things that are not yet done, saying, My counsel shall stand, and I will do all my pleasure: Calling a ravenous bird from the east, the man that executeth my counsel from a far country: yea, I have spoken it, I will also bring it to pass; I have purposed it, I will also do it."

2 Peter 3:9, "The Lord is not slack concerning his promise, as some men count slackness; but is longsuffering to us-ward, not willing that any should perish, but that all should come to repentance."

Psalm 18:30, "As for God, his way is perfect: the word of the LORD is tried: he is a buckler to all those that trust in him."

Jeremiah 33:3, "Call unto me, and I will answer thee, and show thee great and mighty things, which thou knowest not."

Isaiah 55:8-11 For my thoughts are not your thoughts, neither are your ways my ways, saith the LORD. For as the heavens are higher than the earth, so are my ways higher than your ways, and my thoughts than your thoughts. For as the rain cometh down, and the snow from heaven, and returneth not thither, but watereth the earth, and maketh it bring forth and bud, that it may give seed to the sower, and bread to the eater: So shall my word be that goeth forth out of my mouth: it shall not return unto me void, but it shall accomplish that which I please, and it shall prosper in the thing whereto I sent it."

Romans 8:31, "What shall we then say to these things? If God be for us, who can be against us?"

Romans 8:28, "And we know that all things work together for good to them that love God, to them who are the called according to his purpose."

Luke 12:29-31, "And seek not ye what ye shall eat, or what ye shall drink, neither be ye of doubtful mind. For all these things do the nations of the world seek after: and your Father knoweth that ye have need of these things. But rather seek ye the kingdom of God; and all these things shall be added unto you."

Romans 4:20-21, "He staggered not at the promise of God through unbelief; but was strong in faith, giving glory to God; And being fully persuaded that, what he had promised, he was able also to perform."

Isaiah 59:1, "Behold, the LORD'S hand is not shortened, that it cannot save; neither his ear heavy, that it cannot hear:"

1 Thessalonians 5:24, "Faithful is he that calleth you, who also will do it."

1 Peter 4:12-13, "Beloved, think it not strange concerning the fiery trial which is to try you, as though some strange thing happened unto you: But rejoice, inasmuch as ye are partakers of Christ's sufferings; that, when his glory shall be revealed, ye may be glad also with exceeding joy."

❧❧❧ Trouble ❧❧❧

1 Peter 5:7, "Casting all your care upon him; for he careth for you."

2 Corinthians 1:3-4, " Blessed be God, even the Father of our Lord Jesus Christ, the Father of mercies, and the God of all comfort; Who comforteth us in all our tribulation, that we may be able to comfort them which are in any trouble, by the comfort wherewith we ourselves are comforted of God."

Philippians 4:6-7, "Be careful for nothing; but in every thing by prayer and supplication with thanksgiving let your requests be made known unto God. And the peace of God, which passeth all understanding, shall keep your hearts and minds through Christ Jesus."

Nahum 1:7, "The LORD is good, a strong hold in the day of trouble; and he knoweth them that trust in him."

2 Corinthians 4:8-9, "We are troubled on every side, yet not distressed; we are perplexed, but not in despair; Persecuted, but not forsaken; cast down, but not destroyed;"

Psalm 138:7, "Though I walk in the midst of trouble, thou wilt revive me: thou shalt stretch forth thine hand against the wrath of mine enemies, and thy right hand shall save me."

John 14:1, "Let not your heart be troubled: ye believe in God, believe also in me."

Isaiah 43:2, "When thou passest through the waters, I will be with thee; and through the rivers, they shall not overflow thee: when thou walkest through the fire, thou shalt not be burned; neither shall the flame kindle upon thee."

Romans 8:28, "And we know that all things work together for good to them that love God, to them who are the called according to his purpose."

Matthew 6:34, "Take therefore no thought for the morrow: for the morrow shall take thought for the things of itself. Sufficient unto the day is the evil thereof."

Isaiah 51:11, "Therefore the redeemed of the LORD shall return, and come with singing unto Zion; and everlasting joy shall be upon their head: they shall obtain gladness and joy; and sorrow and mourning shall flee away."

John 16:33, "These things I have spoken unto you, that in me ye might have peace. In the world ye shall have tribulation: but be of good cheer; I have overcome the world."

Proverbs 21:23, "Whoso keepeth his mouth and his tongue keepeth his soul from troubles."

ৰ্ত্ত্ত্ত্ত্ত্ত্ব Faithfulness ৰ্ত্ত্ত্ত্ত্ত্ত্ব

Psalm 119:65, "Thou hast dealt well with thy servant, O LORD, according unto thy word."

Joshua 23:14, "And, behold, this day I am going the way of all the earth: and ye know in all your hearts and in all your souls, that not one thing hath failed of all the good things which the LORD your God spake concerning you; all are come to pass unto you, and not one thing hath failed thereof."

Genesis 28:15, "And, behold, I am with thee, and will keep thee in all places whither thou goest, and will bring thee again into this land; for I will not leave thee, until I have done that which I have spoken to thee of."

1 Kings 8:56, "Blessed be the LORD, that hath given rest unto his people Israel, according to all that he promised: there hath not failed one word of all his good promise, which he promised by the hand of Moses his servant."

Psalm 36:5, "Thy mercy, O LORD, is in the heavens; and thy faithfulness reacheth unto the clouds."

Psalm 89:1, "I will sing of the mercies of the LORD for ever: with my mouth will I make known thy faithfulness to all generations."

1 Corinthians 1:9, "God is faithful, by whom ye were called unto the fellowship of his Son Jesus Christ our Lord."

1 Corinthians 10:13, "There hath no temptation taken you but such as is common to man: but God is faithful, who will not suffer you to be tempted above that ye are able; but will with the temptation also make a way to escape, that ye may be able to bear it."

1 Corinthians 10:13, "There hath no temptation taken you but such as is common to man: but God is faithful, who will not suffer you to be tempted above that ye are able; but will with the temptation also make a way to escape, that ye may be able to bear it."

Galatians 6:9, "And let us not be weary in well doing: for in due season we shall reap, if we faint not."

Matthew 25:21, "His lord said unto him, Well done, thou good and faithful servant: thou hast been faithful over a few things, I will make thee ruler over many things: enter thou into the joy of thy lord."

Proverbs 28:20, "A faithful man shall abound with blessings: but he that maketh haste to be rich shall not be innocent."

Proverbs 27:6, "Faithful are the wounds of a friend; but the kisses of an enemy are deceitful."

Revelation 22:6, "And he said unto me, These sayings are faithful and true: and the Lord God of the holy prophets sent his angel to show unto his servants the things which must shortly be done."

1 John 1:9, "If we confess our sins, he is faithful and just to forgive us our sins, and to cleanse us from all unrighteousness."

1 Thessalonians 5:24, "Faithful is he that calleth you, who also will do it."

2 Timothy 2:11, "It is a faithful saying: For if we be dead with him, we shall also live with him:"

1 Corinthians 15:58, "Therefore, my beloved brethren, be ye stedfast, unmoveable, always abounding in the work of the Lord, forasmuch as ye know that your labour is not in vain in the Lord."

Hebrews 10:23, "Let us hold fast the profession of our faith without wavering; (for he is faithful that promised;)"

ঌ৵৶ Godliness ঌ৵৶

1 Timothy 6:6-8, "But godliness with contentment is great gain. For we brought nothing into this world, and it is certain we can carry nothing out. For bodily exercise profiteth little: but godliness is profitable unto all things, having promise of the life that now is, and of that which is to come."

Psalm 4:3, "But know that the LORD hath set apart him that is godly for himself: the LORD will hear when I call unto him."

2 Peter 2:9, "The Lord knoweth how to deliver the godly out of temptations, and to reserve the unjust unto the day of judgment to be punished:"

2 Timothy 3:12, "Yea, and all that will live godly in Christ

Jesus shall suffer persecution."

2 Corinthians 7:1, "Having therefore these promises, dearly beloved, let us cleanse ourselves from all filthiness of the flesh and spirit, perfecting holiness in the fear of God."

Humility

Matthew 23:11-12, "But he that is greatest among you shall be your servant. And whosoever shall exalt himself shall be abased; and he that shall humble himself shall be exalted."

2 Chronicles 7:14, "If my people, which are called by my name, shall humble themselves, and pray, and seek my face, and turn from their wicked ways; then will I hear from heaven, and will forgive their sin, and will heal their land."

Proverbs 6:3, "Do this now, my son, and deliver thyself, when thou art come into the hand of thy friend; go, humble thyself, and make sure thy friend."

James 4:16, "But now ye rejoice in your boastings: all such rejoicing is evil."

1 Peter 5:6, "Humble yourselves therefore under the mighty hand of God, that he may exalt you in due time:"

Proverbs 15:33, "The fear of the LORD is the instruction of wisdom; and before honour is humility."

Proverbs 22:4, "By humility and the fear of the LORD are riches, and honour, and life."

Joy

Proverbs 17:22, "A merry heart doeth good like a medicine: but a broken spirit drieth the bones."

Psalm 16:11, "Thou wilt show me the path of life: in thy presence is fulness of joy; at thy right hand there are pleasures for evermore."

Ecclesiastes 2:26, "For God giveth to a man that is good in his sight wisdom, and knowledge, and joy: but to the sinner he giveth travail, to gather and to heap up, that he may give to him that is good before God. This also is vanity and vexation of spirit."

Isaiah 51:11, "Therefore the redeemed of the LORD shall return, and come with singing unto Zion; and everlasting joy shall be upon their head: they shall obtain gladness and joy; and sorrow and mourning shall flee away."

Luke 2:10, "And the angel said unto them, Fear not: for, behold, I bring you good tidings of great joy, which shall be to all people."

Luke 15:7, "I say unto you, that likewise joy shall be in heaven over one sinner that repenteth, more than over ninety and nine just persons, which need no repentance."

John 15:11, "These things have I spoken unto you, that my joy might remain in you, and that your joy might be full."

❧❧❧ Reaping, Sowing ❧❧❧

Galatians 6:7, "Be not deceived; God is not mocked: for whatsoever a man soweth, that shall he also reap."

Psalm 126:5, "They that sow in tears shall reap in joy."

Matthew 25:26, "His lord answered and said unto him, Thou wicked and slothful servant, thou knewest that I reap where I sowed not, and gather where I have not strowed:"

2 Corinthians 6:9, "As unknown, and yet well known; as dying, and, behold, we live; as chastened, and not killed;"

Galatians 6:8, "For he that soweth to his flesh shall of the flesh reap corruption; but he that soweth to the Spirit shall of the Spirit reap life everlasting."

Work

Proverbs 10:4, "He becometh poor that dealeth with a slack hand: but the hand of the diligent maketh rich."

Proverbs 13:4, "The soul of the sluggard desireth, and hath nothing: but the soul of the diligent shall be made fat."

John 9:4, "I must work the works of him that sent me, while it is day: the night cometh, when no man can work."

Acts 10:35, "But in every nation he that feareth him, and worketh righteousness, is accepted with him."

Proverbs 16:3, "Commit thy works unto the LORD, and thy thoughts shall be established."

Peace

Isaiah 26:3, "Thou wilt keep him in perfect peace, whose mind is stayed on thee: because he trusteth in thee."

Ephesians 2:13-14 "But now in Christ Jesus ye who sometimes were far off are made nigh by the blood of Christ. For he is our peace, who hath made both one, and hath broken down the middle wall of partition between us;"

Romans 16:20, "And the God of peace shall bruise Satan under your feet shortly. The grace of our Lord Jesus Christ be with you. Amen."

Isaiah 26:12, "LORD, thou wilt ordain peace for us: for thou also hast wrought all our works in us."

Philippians 4:9, "Those things, which ye have both learned, and received, and heard, and seen in me, do: and the God of peace shall be with you."

Romans 5:1, "Therefore being justified by faith, we have peace with God through our Lord Jesus Christ:"

Psalm 4:8, "I will both lay me down in peace, and sleep: for thou, LORD, only makest me dwell in safety."

Psalm 29:11, "The LORD will give strength unto his people; the LORD will bless his people with peace."

Philippians 4:6-7 "Be careful for nothing; but in every thing by prayer and supplication with thanksgiving let your requests be made known unto God. And the peace of God, which passeth all understanding, shall keep your hearts and minds through Christ Jesus."

❧❧❧ Righteousness ❧❧❧

2 Corinthians 5:21, "For he hath made him to be sin for us, who knew no sin; that we might be made the righteousness of God in him."

Galatians 3:6-7, "Even as Abraham believed God, and it was accounted to him for righteousness. Know ye therefore that they which are of faith, the same are the children of Abraham."

Romans 4:5, "But to him that worketh not, but believeth on him that justifieth the ungodly, his faith is counted for righteousness."

Romans 5:17, "For if by one man's offence death reigned by one; much more they which receive abundance of grace and of the gift of righteousness shall reign in life by one, Jesus Christ."

Romans 8:10, "And if Christ be in you, the body is dead

because of sin; but the Spirit is life because of righteousness."

Romans 8:3-4, "For what the law could not do, in that it was weak through the flesh, God sending his own Son in the likeness of sinful flesh, and for sin, condemned sin in the flesh: That the righteousness of the law might be fulfilled in us, who walk not after the flesh, but after the Spirit."

Romans 10:10, "For with the heart man believeth unto righteousness; and with the mouth confession is made unto salvation."

Isaiah 33:17, "Thine eyes shall see the king in his beauty: they shall behold the land that is very far off."

ಬಡ್ಡಿ Strength ಬಡ್ಡಿ

Isaiah 30:15, "For thus saith the Lord GOD, the Holy One of Israel; In returning and rest shall ye be saved; in quietness and in confidence shall be your strength: and ye would not."

Colossians 1:10-12, "That ye might walk worthy of the Lord unto all pleasing, being fruitful in every good work, and increasing in the knowledge of God; Strengthened with all might, according to his glorious power, unto all patience and longsuffering with joyfulness; Giving thanks unto the Father, which hath made us meet to be partakers of the inheritance of the saints in light:"

Isaiah 40:31, "But they that wait upon the LORD shall renew their strength; they shall mount up with wings as eagles; they shall run, and not be weary; and they shall walk, and not faint."

Nehemiah 8:10, "Then he said unto them, Go your way, eat the fat, and drink the sweet, and send portions unto them for whom nothing is prepared: for this day is holy unto our Lord: neither be ye sorry; for the joy of the LORD is your strength."

Philippians 4:13, "I can do all things through Christ which strengtheneth me."

Isaiah 41:10, "Fear thou not; for I am with thee: be not dismayed; for I am thy God: I will strengthen thee; yea, I will help thee; yea, I will uphold thee with the right hand of my righteousness."

Proverbs 8:14, "Counsel is mine, and sound wisdom: I am understanding; I have strength."

Isaiah 40:29, "He giveth power to the faint; and to them that have no might he increaseth strength."

Depression

Psalm 34:17, "The righteous cry, and the LORD heareth, and delivereth them out of all their troubles."

Isaiah 43:2, "When thou passest through the waters, I will be with thee; and through the rivers, they shall not overflow thee: when thou walkest through the fire, thou shalt not be burned; neither shall the flame kindle upon thee."

2 Corinthians 1:3-4, "Blessed be God, even the Father of our Lord Jesus Christ, the Father of mercies, and the God of all comfort; Who comforteth us in all our tribulation, that we may be able to comfort them which are in any trouble, by the comfort wherewith we ourselves are comforted of God."

Psalm 147:3, "He healeth the broken in heart, and bindeth up their wounds."

Psalm 30:5, "For his anger endureth but a moment; in his favour is life: weeping may endure for a night, but joy cometh in the morning."

1 Peter 4:12, "Beloved, think it not strange concerning the fiery trial which is to try you, as though some strange thing happened unto you:"

Isaiah 41:10, "Fear thou not; for I am with thee: be not dismayed; for I am thy God: I will strengthen thee; yea, I will help thee; yea, I will uphold thee with the right hand of my righteousness."

1 Peter 5:6-7, "Humble yourselves therefore under the mighty hand of God, that he may exalt you in due time: Casting all your care upon him; for he careth for you."

Isaiah 51:11, "Therefore the redeemed of the LORD shall return, and come with singing unto Zion; and everlasting joy shall be upon their head: they shall obtain gladness and joy; and sorrow and mourning shall flee away."

Romans 8:38-39, "For I am persuaded, that neither death, nor life, nor angels, nor principalities, nor powers, nor things present, nor things to come, Nor height, nor depth, nor any other creature, shall be able to separate us from the love of God, which is in Christ Jesus our Lord."

ঔক্ষ্ণ Contentment ঔক্ষ্ণ

Psalm 34:10, "The young lions do lack, and suffer hunger: but they that seek the LORD shall not want any good thing."

Psalm 37:3, "Trust in the LORD, and do good; so shalt thou dwell in the land, and verily thou shalt be fed."

Psalm 103:1-5, "A Psalm of David. Bless the LORD, O my soul: and all that is within me, bless his holy name. Bless the LORD, O my soul, and forget not all his benefits: Who forgiveth all thine iniquities; who healeth all thy diseases; Who redeemeth thy life from destruction; who crowneth thee with lovingkindness and tender mercies; Who satisfieth thy mouth with good things; so that thy youth is renewed like the eagle's."

Philippians 4:12, "I know both how to be abased, and I know how to abound: every where and in all things I am instructed both to be full and to be hungry, both to abound and to suffer need."

Psalm 63:5, "My soul shall be satisfied as with marrow and fatness; and my mouth shall praise thee with joyful lips:"

Psalm 107:9, "For he satisfieth the longing soul, and filleth the hungry soul with goodness."

Proverbs 12:14, "A man shall be satisfied with good by the fruit of his mouth: and the recompense of a man's hands shall be rendered unto him."

2 Corinthians 9:8, "And God is able to make all grace abound toward you; that ye, always having all sufficiency in all things, may abound to every good work:"

Matthew 5:6, "Blessed are they which do hunger and thirst after righteousness: for they shall be filled."

ೋೀೀ Anger ೋೀೀ

James 1:19-20, "Wherefore, my beloved brethren, let every man be swift to hear, slow to speak, slow to wrath: For the wrath of man worketh not the righteousness of God."

Proverbs 15:1, "A soft answer turneth away wrath: but grievous words stir up anger."

Matthew 6:14, "For if ye forgive men their trespasses, your heavenly Father will also forgive you:"

Romans 12:19, "Dearly beloved, avenge not yourselves, but rather give place unto wrath: for it is written, Vengeance is mine; I will repay, saith the Lord."

Hebrews 10:30, "For we know him that hath said,

Vengeance belongeth unto me, I will recompense, saith the Lord. And again, The Lord shall judge his people."

◈◈◈ Submission ◈◈◈

Hebrews 13:17, "Obey them that have the rule over you, and submit yourselves: for they watch for your souls, as they that must give account, that they may do it with joy, and not with grief: for that is unprofitable for you."

1 Peter 2:13-15, "Submit yourselves to every ordinance of man for the Lord's sake: whether it be to the king, as supreme; Or unto governors, as unto them that are sent by him for the punishment of evildoers, and for the praise of them that do well. For so is the will of God, that with well doing ye may put to silence the ignorance of foolish men:"

James 4:7, "Submit yourselves therefore to God. Resist the devil, and he will flee from you."

Isaiah 1:19-20, "If ye be willing and obedient, ye shall eat the good of the land: But if ye refuse and rebel, ye shall be devoured with the sword: for the mouth of the LORD hath spoken it."

1 Peter 5:5-6, "Likewise, ye younger, submit yourselves unto the elder. Yea, all of you be subject one to another, and be clothed with humility: for God resisteth the proud, and giveth grace to the humble. Humble yourselves therefore under the mighty hand of God, that he may exalt you in due time:"

◈◈◈ Backsliding ◈◈◈

Revelation 3:2, "Be watchful, and strengthen the things which remain, that are ready to die: for I have not found thy works perfect before God."

Revelation 3:15-16, "I know thy works, that thou art

neither cold nor hot: I would thou wert cold or hot. So then because thou art lukewarm, and neither cold nor hot, I will spue thee out of my mouth."

1 John 1:9, "If we confess our sins, he is faithful and just to forgive us our sins, and to cleanse us from all unrighteousness."

Psalm 44:20-21, "If we have forgotten the name of our God, or stretched out our hands to a strange god; Shall not God search this out? for he knoweth the secrets of the heart."

Malachi 3:7a, "Even from the days of your fathers ye are gone away from mine ordinances, and have not kept them."

❦❧ Sorrow, Grief ❦❧

1 Thessalonians 4:13-14, "But I would not have you to be ignorant, brethren, concerning them which are asleep, that ye sorrow not, even as others which have no hope. For if we believe that Jesus died and rose again, even so them also which sleep in Jesus will God bring with him."

Isaiah 49:13b, "...for the LORD hath comforted his people, and will have mercy upon his afflicted."

2 Thessalonians 2:16-17, "Now our Lord Jesus Christ himself, and God, even our Father, which hath loved us, and hath given us everlasting consolation and good hope through grace, Comfort your hearts, and stablish you in every good word and work."

Isaiah 41:10, "Fear thou not; for I am with thee: be not dismayed; for I am thy God: I will strengthen thee; yea, I will help thee; yea, I will uphold thee with the right hand of my righteousness."

Isaiah 43:2, "When thou passest through the waters, I will be with thee; and through the rivers, they shall not overflow thee: when thou walkest through the fire, thou shalt not be burned; neither shall the flame kindle upon thee."

2 Corinthians 1:3-4, "Blessed be God, even the Father of our Lord Jesus Christ, the Father of mercies, and the God of all comfort; Who comforteth us in all our tribulation, that we may be able to comfort them which are in any trouble, by the comfort wherewith we ourselves are comforted of God."

1 Peter 5:7, "Casting all your care upon him; for he careth for you."

Revelation 21:4, "And God shall wipe away all tears from their eyes; and there shall be no more death, neither sorrow, nor crying, neither shall there be any more pain: for the former things are passed away."

Matthew 5:4, "Blessed are they that mourn: for they shall be comforted."

1 Corinthians 15:57, "But thanks be to God, which giveth us the victory through our Lord Jesus Christ."

Psalm 23:4, "Yea, though I walk through the valley of the shadow of death, I will fear no evil: for thou art with me; thy rod and thy staff they comfort me."

✧✦✧ Financial ✧✦✧

Psalm 23:1, "A Psalm of David. The LORD is my shepherd; I shall not want."

Psalm 34:10, "The young lions do lack, and suffer hunger: but they that seek the LORD shall not want any good thing."

Deuteronomy 28:2, "And all these blessings shall come on thee, and overtake thee, if thou shalt hearken unto the voice of the LORD thy God."

Luke 6:38, "Give, and it shall be given unto you; good

measure, pressed down, and shaken together, and running over, shall men give into your bosom. For with the same measure that ye mete withal it shall be measured to you again."

2 Corinthians 9:6-8, "But this I say, He which soweth sparingly shall reap also sparingly; and he which soweth bountifully shall reap also bountifully. Every man according as he purposeth in his heart, so let him give; not grudgingly, or of necessity: for God loveth a cheerful giver. And God is able to make all grace abound toward you; that ye, always having all sufficiency in all things, may abound to every good work:"

Matthew 19:29, "And every one that hath forsaken houses, or brethren, or sisters, or father, or mother, or wife, or children, or lands, for my name's sake, shall receive an hundredfold, and shall inherit everlasting life."

Malachi 3:10, "Bring ye all the tithes into the storehouse, that there may be meat in mine house, and prove me now herewith, saith the LORD of hosts, if I will not open you the windows of heaven, and pour you out a blessing, that there shall not be room enough to receive it."

Joshua 1:8, "This book of the law shall not depart out of thy mouth; but thou shalt meditate therein day and night, that thou mayest observe to do according to all that is written therein: for then thou shalt make thy way prosperous, and then thou shalt have good success."

Matthew 6:31-33, "Therefore take no thought, saying, What shall we eat? or, What shall we drink? or, Wherewithal shall we be clothed? (For after all these things do the Gentiles seek:) for your heavenly Father knoweth that ye have need of all these things. But seek ye first the kingdom of God, and his righteousness; and all these things shall be added unto you."

Philippians 4:19, "But my God shall supply all your need according to his riches in glory by Christ Jesus."

faith

Hebrews 11:1, "Now faith is the substance of things hoped for, the evidence of things not seen."

Mark 11:22-24, "And Jesus answering saith unto them, Have faith in God. For verily I say unto you, That whosoever shall say unto this mountain, Be thou removed, and be thou cast into the sea; and shall not doubt in his heart, but shall believe that those things which he saith shall come to pass; he shall have whatsoever he saith. Therefore I say unto you, What things soever ye desire, when ye pray, believe that ye receive them, and ye shall have them."

1 Peter 1:7-9, "That the trial of your faith, being much more precious than of gold that perisheth, though it be tried with fire, might be found unto praise and honour and glory at the appearing of Jesus Christ: Whom having not seen, ye love; in whom, though now ye see him not, yet believing, ye rejoice with joy unspeakable and full of glory: Receiving the end of your faith, even the salvation of your souls."

Mark 9:23, "Jesus said unto him, If thou canst believe, all things are possible to him that believeth."

Romans 10:17, "So then faith cometh by hearing, and hearing by the word of God."

Romans 1:17, "For therein is the righteousness of God revealed from faith to faith: as it is written, The just shall live by faith."

Matthew 9:20-22, "And, behold, a woman, which was diseased with an issue of blood twelve years, came behind him, and touched the hem of his garment: For she said within herself, If I may but touch his garment, I shall be whole. But Jesus turned him about, and when he saw her, he said, Daughter, be of good comfort; thy faith hath made thee whole. And the woman was made whole from that hour."

Matthew 17:20, "And Jesus said unto them, Because of your unbelief: for verily I say unto you, If ye have faith as a grain of mustard seed, ye shall say unto this mountain, Remove hence to yonder place; and it shall remove; and nothing shall be impossible unto you."

1 John 1:7-9, "But if we walk in the light, as he is in the light, we have fellowship one with another, and the blood of Jesus Christ his Son cleanseth us from all sin. If we say that we have no sin, we deceive ourselves, and the truth is not in us. If we confess our sins, he is faithful and just to forgive us our sins, and to cleanse us from all unrighteousness."

John 15:15a, "Henceforth I call you not servants; for the servant knoweth not what his lord doeth: but I have called you friends; "

~~ Eternity ~~

John 11:25-26, "Jesus said unto her, I am the resurrection, and the life: he that believeth in me, though he were dead, yet shall he live: And whosoever liveth and believeth in me shall never die. Believest thou this?"

1 John 5:11, "And this is the record, that God hath given to us eternal life, and this life is in his Son."

John 5:24, "Verily, verily, I say unto you, He that heareth my word, and believeth on him that sent me, hath everlasting life, and shall not come into condemnation; but is passed from death unto life."

John 10:27-28, "My sheep hear my voice, and I know them, and they follow me: And I give unto them eternal life; and they shall never perish, neither shall any man pluck them out of my hand."

John 6:47, "Verily, verily, I say unto you, He that believeth on me hath everlasting life."

Psalm 37:18, "The LORD knoweth the days of the upright: and their inheritance shall be for ever."

John 4:14, "But whosoever drinketh of the water that I shall give him shall never thirst; but the water that I shall give him shall be in him a well of water springing up into everlasting life."

Psalm 23:6, "Surely goodness and mercy shall follow me all the days of my life: and I will dwell in the house of the LORD for ever."

John 6:51, "I am the living bread which came down from heaven: if any man eat of this bread, he shall live for ever: and the bread that I will give is my flesh, which I will give for the life of the world."

൴ Obedience ൴

Deuteronomy 11:26-28, "Behold, I set before you this day a blessing and a curse; A blessing, if ye obey the commandments of the LORD your God, which I command you this day: And a curse, if ye will not obey the commandments of the LORD your God, but turn aside out of the way which I command you this day, to go after other gods, which ye have not known."

1 John 2:3-6, "And hereby we do know that we know him, if we keep his commandments. He that saith, I know him, and keepeth not his commandments, is a liar, and the truth is not in him. But whoso keepeth his word, in him verily is the love of God perfected: hereby know we that we are in him. He that saith he abideth in him ought himself also so to walk, even as he walked."

Jeremiah 7:23, "But this thing commanded I them, saying, Obey my voice, and I will be your God, and ye shall be my people: and walk ye in all the ways that I have commanded you, that it may be well unto you."

1 Kings 3:14, "And if thou wilt walk in my ways, to keep my statutes and my commandments, as thy father David did walk, then I will lengthen thy days."

John 14:15, "If ye love me, keep my commandments."

Colossians 3:22-24, "Servants, obey in all things your masters according to the flesh; not with eyeservice, as menpleasers; but in singleness of heart, fearing God: And whatsoever ye do, do it heartily, as to the Lord, and not unto men; Knowing that of the Lord ye shall receive the reward of the inheritance: for ye serve the Lord Christ."

ಹಇತ God's Grace ಹಇತ

Psalm 84:11, "For the LORD God is a sun and shield: the LORD will give grace and glory: no good thing will he withhold from them that walk uprightly."

Exodus 33:17, "And the LORD said unto Moses, I will do this thing also that thou hast spoken: for thou hast found grace in my sight, and I know thee by name."

Psalm 55:12, "For it was not an enemy that reproached me; then I could have borne it: neither was it he that hated me that did magnify himself against me; then I would have hid myself from him:"

Proverbs 14:9, "Fools make a mock at sin: but among the righteous there is favour."

Hebrews 4:16, "Let us therefore come boldly unto the throne of grace, that we may obtain mercy, and find grace to help in time of need."

Ephesians 2:8-9, "For by grace are ye saved through faith; and that not of yourselves: it is the gift of God: Not of works, lest any man should boast."

The Holy Spirit

Romans 5:5, "And hope maketh not ashamed; because the love of God is shed abroad in our hearts by the Holy Ghost which is given unto us."

John 14:16-17, "And I will pray the Father, and he shall give you another Comforter, that he may abide with you for ever; Even the Spirit of truth; whom the world cannot receive, because it seeth him not, neither knoweth him: but ye know him; for he dwelleth with you, and shall be in you."

John 16:7,13, Nevertheless I tell you the truth; It is expedient for you that I go away: for if I go not away, the Comforter will not come unto you; but if I depart, I will send him unto you. Howbeit when he, the Spirit of truth, is come, he will guide you into all truth: for he shall not speak of himself; but whatsoever he shall hear, that shall he speak: and he will show you things to come."

Matthew 3:11, "I indeed baptize you with water unto repentance: but he that cometh after me is mightier than I, whose shoes I am not worthy to bear: he shall baptize you with the Holy Ghost, and with fire:"

Joel 2:28, "And it shall come to pass afterward, that I will pour out my spirit upon all flesh; and your sons and your daughters shall prophesy, your old men shall dream dreams, your young men shall see visions:"

Acts 2:38, "Then Peter said unto them, Repent, and be baptized every one of you in the name of Jesus Christ for the remission of sins, and ye shall receive the gift of the Holy Ghost."

Luke 11:13, "If ye then, being evil, know how to give good gifts unto your children: how much more shall your heavenly Father give the Holy Spirit to them that ask him?"

The Church

Ephesians 1:10, "That in the dispensation of the fulness of times he might gather together in one all things in Christ, both which are in heaven, and which are on earth; even in him:"

Ephesians 1:22-23, "And hath put all things under his feet, and gave him to be the head over all things to the church, Which is his body, the fulness of him that filleth all in all."

Matthew 16:15-18, "He saith unto them, But whom say ye that I am? And Simon Peter answered and said, Thou art the Christ, the Son of the living God. And Jesus answered and said unto him, Blessed art thou, Simon Barjona: for flesh and blood hath not revealed it unto thee, but my Father which is in heaven. And I say also unto thee, That thou art Peter, and upon this rock I will build my church; and the gates of hell shall not prevail against it."

Psalm 133:1, "A Song of degrees of David. Behold, how good and how pleasant it is for brethren to dwell together in unity!"

Ephesians 2:20-22, "And are built upon the foundation of the apostles and prophets, Jesus Christ himself being the chief corner stone; In whom all the building fitly framed together groweth unto an holy temple in the Lord: In whom ye also are builded together for an habitation of God through the Spirit."

Ephesians 4:11-12, "And he gave some, apostles; and some, prophets; and some, evangelists; and some, pastors and teachers; For the perfecting of the saints, for the work of the ministry, for the edifying of the body of Christ:"

Giving, Stewardship

Malachi 3:8-12, "Will a man rob God? Yet ye have robbed me. But ye say, Wherein have we robbed thee? In tithes and offerings. Ye are cursed with a curse: for ye have robbed me, even this whole nation. Bring ye all the tithes into the storehouse, that there may be meat in mine house, and prove me now herewith, saith the LORD of hosts, if I will not open you the windows of heaven, and pour you out a blessing, that there shall not be room enough to receive it. And I will rebuke the devourer for your sakes, and he shall not destroy the fruits of your ground; neither shall your vine cast her fruit before the time in the field, saith the LORD of hosts. And all nations shall call you blessed: for ye shall be a delightsome land, saith the LORD of hosts."

2 Corinthains 9:6-8, "But this I say, He which soweth sparingly shall reap also sparingly; and he which soweth bountifully shall reap also bountifully. Every man according as he purposeth in his heart, so let him give; not grudgingly, or of necessity: for God loveth a cheerful giver. And God is able to make all grace abound toward you; that ye, always having all sufficiency in all things, may abound to every good work:"

Matthew 6:33, "But seek ye first the kingdom of God, and his righteousness; and all these things shall be added unto you."

Luke 6:38, "Give, and it shall be given unto you; good measure, pressed down, and shaken together, and running over, shall men give into your bosom. For with the same measure that ye mete withal it shall be measured to you again."

Matthew 19:29, "And every one that hath forsaken houses, or brethren, or sisters, or father, or mother, or wife, or children, or lands, for my name's sake, shall receive an hundredfold, and shall inherit everlasting life."

Deuteronomy 28:2, "And all these blessings shall come on thee, and overtake thee, if thou shalt hearken unto the voice of the LORD thy God."

Proverbs 11:24-25, "There is that scattereth, and yet increaseth; and there is that withholdeth more than is meet, but it tendeth to poverty. The liberal soul shall be made fat: and he that watereth shall be watered also himself."

Mark 10:29-30, "And Jesus answered and said, Verily I say unto you, There is no man that hath left house, or brethren, or sisters, or father, or mother, or wife, or children, or lands, for my sake, and the gospel's, But he shall receive an hundredfold now in this time, houses, and brethren, and sisters, and mothers, and children, and lands, with persecutions; and in the world to come eternal life."

Joshua 1:8, "This book of the law shall not depart out of thy mouth; but thou shalt meditate therein day and night, that thou mayest observe to do according to all that is written therein: for then thou shalt make thy way prosperous, and then thou shalt have good success."

ങ‌ൟ‌ൖ Satan ങ‌ൟ‌ൖ

Revelation 12:11, "And they overcame him by the blood of the Lamb, and by the word of their testimony; and they loved not their lives unto the death."

Colossians 1:13, "Who hath delivered us from the power of darkness, and hath translated us into the kingdom of his dear Son:"

Proverbs 18:10, "The name of the LORD is a strong tower: the righteous runneth into it, and is safe."

Colossians 2:10, 15 "And ye are complete in him, which is the head of all principality and power: And having spoiled principalities and powers, he made a show of them openly, triumphing over them in it."

James 4:7, "Submit yourselves therefore to God. Resist the devil, and he will flee from you."

1 John 3:8, "He that committeth sin is of the devil; for the devil sinneth from the beginning. For this purpose the Son of God was manifested, that he might destroy the works of the devil."

1 John 4:4, "Ye are of God, little children, and have overcome them: because greater is he that is in you, than he that is in the world."

2 Corinthians 10:3-5, "For though we walk in the flesh, we do not war after the flesh: (For the weapons of our warfare are not carnal, but mighty through God to the pulling down of strong holds;) Casting down imaginations, and every high thing that exalteth itself against the knowledge of God, and bringing into captivity every thought to the obedience of Christ;"

Romans 16:20, "And the God of peace shall bruise Satan under your feet shortly. The grace of our Lord Jesus Christ be with you. Amen."

The Second Coming

1 Thessalonians 4:13-18, "But I would not have you to be ignorant, brethren, concerning them which are asleep, that ye sorrow not, even as others which have no hope. For if we believe that Jesus died and rose again, even so them also which sleep in Jesus will God bring with him. For this we say unto you by the word of the Lord, that we which are alive and remain unto the coming of the Lord shall not prevent them which are asleep. For the Lord himself shall descend from heaven with a shout, with the voice of the archangel, and with the trump of God: and the dead in Christ shall rise first: Then we which are alive and remain shall be caught up together with them in the clouds, to meet the Lord in the air: and so shall we ever be with the Lord. Wherefore comfort one another with these words."

Acts 1:11, "Which also said, Ye men of Galilee, why stand ye gazing up into heaven? this same Jesus, which is taken up from you into heaven, shall so come in like manner as ye have seen him go into heaven."

1 John 3:2-3, "Beloved, now are we the sons of God, and it doth not yet appear what we shall be: but we know that, when he shall appear, we shall be like him; for we shall see him as he is. And every man that hath this hope in him purifieth himself, even as he is pure."

1 Corinthians 15:51-57, "Behold, I show you a mystery; We shall not all sleep, but we shall all be changed, In a moment, in the twinkling of an eye, at the last trump: for the trumpet shall sound, and the dead shall be raised incorruptible, and we shall be changed. For this corruptible must put on incorruption, and this mortal must put on immortality. So when this corruptible shall have put on incorruption, and this mortal shall have put on immortality, then shall be brought to pass the saying that is written, Death is swallowed up in victory. O death, where is thy sting? O grave, where is thy victory? The sting of death is sin; and the strength of sin is the law. But thanks be to God, which giveth us the victory through our Lord Jesus Christ.

Matthew 24:36, "But of that day and hour knoweth no man, no, not the angels of heaven, but my Father only."

2 Timothy 3:1, "This know also, that in the last days perilous times shall come."

John 14:1-4, "Let not your heart be troubled: ye believe in God, believe also in me. In my Father's house are many mansions: if it were not so, I would have told you. I go to prepare a place for you. And if I go and prepare a place for you, I will come again, and receive you unto myself; that where I am, there ye may be also. And whither I go ye know, and the way ye know."

Matthew 24:34, "Verily I say unto you, This generation shall not pass, till all these things be fulfilled."

Fellowship

1 John 1:3, 7, "That which we have seen and heard declare we unto you, that ye also may have fellowship with us: and truly our fellowship is with the Father, and with his Son Jesus Christ. But if we walk in the light, as he is in the light, we have fellowship one with another, and the blood of Jesus Christ his Son cleanseth us from all sin."

Romans 15:5-7, "Now the God of patience and consolation grant you to be likeminded one toward another according to Christ Jesus: That ye may with one mind and one mouth glorify God, even the Father of our Lord Jesus Christ. Wherefore receive ye one another, as Christ also received us to the glory of God."

Ephesians 2:19-22, "Now therefore ye are no more strangers and foreigners, but fellowcitizens with the saints, and of the household of God; And are built upon the foundation of the apostles and prophets, Jesus Christ himself being the chief corner stone; In whom all the building fitly framed together groweth unto an holy temple in the Lord: In whom ye also are builded together for an habitation of God through the Spirit."

Revelation 3:20, "Behold, I stand at the door, and knock: if any man hear my voice, and open the door, I will come in to him, and will sup with him, and he with me."

John 14:23, "Jesus answered and said unto him, If a man love me, he will keep my words: and my Father will love him, and we will come unto him, and make our abode with him."

Psalm 119:63, "I am a companion of all them that fear thee, and of them that keep thy precepts."

John 15:4-5, 7, "Abide in me, and I in you. As the branch cannot bear fruit of itself, except it abide in the vine; no more can ye, except ye abide in me. I am the vine, ye are the branches: He that abideth in me, and I in him, the same bringeth forth much fruit: for without me ye can do nothing. If ye abide in me, and my words abide in you, ye shall ask what ye will, and it shall be done unto you."

John 14:21, "He that hath my commandments, and keepeth them, he it is that loveth me: and he that loveth me shall be loved of my Father, and I will love him, and will manifest myself to him."

1 Corinthians 1:9, "God is faithful, by whom ye were called unto the fellowship of his Son Jesus Christ our Lord."

Matthew 18:20, "For where two or three are gathered together in my name, there am I in the midst of them."

Psalm 119:63, "I am a companion of all them that fear thee, and of them that keep thy precepts."

John 14:18, "I will not leave you comfortless: I will come to you."

❧❧❧ Marriage ❧❧❧

Hebrews 13:4, "Marriage is honourable in all, and the bed undefiled: but whoremongers and adulterers God will judge."

Genesis 2:24, "Therefore shall a man leave his father and his mother, and shall cleave unto his wife: and they shall be one flesh."

1 Peter 3:7, "Likewise, ye husbands, dwell with them according to knowledge, giving honour unto the wife, as unto the weaker vessel, and as being heirs together of the grace of life; that your prayers be not hindered."

Jeremiah 29:6, "Take ye wives, and beget sons and daughters; and take wives for your sons, and give your daughters to husbands, that they may bear sons and daughters; that ye may be increased there, and not diminished."

1 Peter 3:1, "Likewise, ye wives, be in subjection to your own husbands; that, if any obey not the word, they also may without the word be won by the conversation of the wives;"

❦❧ Family ❦❧

Acts 16:31, "And they said, Believe on the Lord Jesus Christ, and thou shalt be saved, and thy house."

Proverbs 22:6, "Train up a child in the way he should go: and when he is old, he will not depart from it."

Proverbs 29:17, "Correct thy son, and he shall give thee rest; yea, he shall give delight unto thy soul."

Proverbs 23:24, "The father of the righteous shall greatly rejoice: and he that begetteth a wise child shall have joy of him."

Exodus 20:12, "Honour thy father and thy mother: that thy days may be long upon the land which the LORD thy God giveth thee."

Psalm 127:3-5, "Lo, children are an heritage of the LORD: and the fruit of the womb is his reward. As arrows are in the hand of a mighty man; so are children of the youth. Happy is the man that hath his quiver full of them: they shall not be ashamed, but they shall speak with the enemies in the gate."

Proverbs 13:22, "A good man leaveth an inheritance to his children's children: and the wealth of the sinner is laid up for the just."

Isaiah 54:13, "And all thy children shall be taught of the LORD; and great shall be the peace of thy children."

Malachi 4:6, "And he shall turn the heart of the fathers to the children, and the heart of the children to their fathers, lest I come and smite the earth with a curse."

Proverbs 17:6, "Children's children are the crown of old men; and the glory of children are their fathers."

Psalm 128:1-4, "Blessed is every one that feareth the LORD; that walketh in his ways. For thou shalt eat the labour of thine hands: happy shalt thou be, and it shall be well with thee. Thy wife shall be as a fruitful vine by the sides of thine house: thy children like olive plants round about thy table. Behold, that thus shall the man be blessed that feareth the LORD."

◈◈◈ Widows ◈◈◈

Job 29:13, "The blessing of him that was ready to perish came upon me: and I caused the widow's heart to sing for joy."

Proverbs 15:25, "The LORD will destroy the house of the proud: but he will establish the border of the widow."

Psalm 147:3, "He healeth the broken in heart, and bindeth up their wounds."

Psalm 146:9, "The LORD preserveth the strangers; he relieveth the fatherless and widow: but the way of the wicked he turneth upside down."

Jeremiah 49:11, "Leave thy fatherless children, I will preserve them alive; and let thy widows trust in me."

John 14:18, "I will not leave you comfortless: I will come to you."

John 16:22, "And ye now therefore have sorrow: but I will see you again, and your heart shall rejoice, and your joy no man taketh from you."

Single People

1 Corinthians 7:8, "I say therefore to the unmarried and widows, It is good for them if they abide even as I."

1 Corinthians 7:27-28, "Art thou bound unto a wife? seek not to be loosed. Art thou loosed from a wife? seek not a wife. But and if thou marry, thou hast not sinned; and if a virgin marry, she hath not sinned. Nevertheless such shall have trouble in the flesh: but I spare you."

Galatians 6:4, "But let every man prove his own work, and then shall he have rejoicing in himself alone, and not in another."

1 Corinthians 7:32, 33, 35, "But I would have you without carefulness. He that is unmarried careth for the things that belong to the Lord, how he may please the Lord: But he that is married careth for the things that are of the world, how he may please his wife. And this I speak for your own profit; not that I may cast a snare upon you, but for that which is comely, and that ye may attend upon the Lord without distraction."

Proverbs 3:5-6, "Trust in the LORD with all thine heart; and lean not unto thine own understanding. In all thy ways acknowledge him, and he shall direct thy paths."

2 Peter 1:6-8, "And to knowledge temperance; and to temperance patience; and to patience godliness; And to godliness brotherly kindness; and to brotherly kindness charity. For if these things be in you, and abound, they make you that ye shall neither be barren nor unfruitful in the knowledge of our Lord Jesus Christ."

Psalm 37:4, "Delight thyself also in the LORD; and he shall give thee the desires of thine heart."

Elderly

Isaiah 46:4, "And even to your old age I am he; and even to hoar hairs will I carry you: I have made, and I will bear; even I will carry, and will deliver you."

Psalm 92:14, "They shall still bring forth fruit in old age; they shall be fat and flourishing;"

Romans 8:38-39, "For I am persuaded, that neither death, nor life, nor angels, nor principalities, nor powers, nor things present, nor things to come, Nor height, nor depth, nor any other creature, shall be able to separate us from the love of God, which is in Christ Jesus our Lord."

Proverbs 3:2, "For length of days, and long life, and peace, shall they add to thee."

Psalm 91:16, "With long life will I satisfy him, and show him my salvation."

Isaiah 64:4, "For since the beginning of the world men have not heard, nor perceived by the ear, neither hath the eye seen, O God, beside thee, what he hath prepared for him that waiteth for him."

Hebrews 13:5, "Let your conversation be without covetousness; and be content with such things as ye have: for he hath said, I will never leave thee, nor forsake thee."

Psalm 23:4, 6, "Yea, though I walk through the valley of the shadow of death, I will fear no evil: for thou art with me; thy rod and thy staff they comfort me. Surely goodness and mercy shall follow me all the days of my life: and I will dwell in the house of the LORD for ever."

Isaiah 41:17, "When the poor and needy seek water, and there is none, and their tongue faileth for thirst, I the LORD will hear them, I the God of Israel will not forsake them."

Influence

Matthew 5:14-16, "Ye are the light of the world. A city that is set on an hill cannot be hid. Neither do men light a candle, and put it under a bushel, but on a candlestick; and it giveth light unto all that are in the house. Let your light so shine before men, that they may see your good works, and glorify your Father which is in heaven."

Daniel 12:3, "And they that be wise shall shine as the brightness of the firmament; and they that turn many to righteousness as the stars for ever and ever."

Acts 1:8, "But ye shall receive power, after that the Holy Ghost is come upon you: and ye shall be witnesses unto me both in Jerusalem, and in all Judaea, and in Samaria, and unto the uttermost part of the earth."

Matthew 28:19-20, "Go ye therefore, and teach all nations, baptizing them in the name of the Father, and of the Son, and of the Holy Ghost: Teaching them to observe all things whatsoever I have commanded you: and, lo, I am with you alway, even unto the end of the world. Amen."

John 14:12, "Verily, verily, I say unto you, He that believeth on me, the works that I do shall he do also; and greater works than these shall he do; because I go unto my Father."

Matthew 16:18-19, "And I say also unto thee, That thou art Peter, and upon this rock I will build my church; and the gates of hell shall not prevail against it. And I will give unto thee the keys of the kingdom of heaven: and whatsoever thou shalt bind on earth shall be bound in heaven: and whatsoever thou shalt loose on earth shall be loosed in heaven."

1 John 5:4-5, "For whatsoever is born of God overcometh the world: and this is the victory that overcometh the world, even our faith. Who is he that overcometh the world, but he that believeth that Jesus is the Son of God?"

Prosperity

Joshua 1:8, "This book of the law shall not depart out of thy mouth; but thou shalt meditate therein day and night, that thou mayest observe to do according to all that is written therein: for then thou shalt make thy way prosperous, and then thou shalt have good success."

Isaiah 48:17, "Thus saith the LORD, thy Redeemer, the Holy One of Israel; I am the LORD thy God which teacheth thee to profit, which leadeth thee by the way that thou shouldest go."

Deuteronomy 28:1, "And it shall come to pass, if thou shalt hearken diligently unto the voice of the LORD thy God, to observe and to do all his commandments which I command thee this day, that the LORD thy God will set thee on high above all nations of the earth:"

Deuteronomy 8:18, "But thou shalt remember the LORD thy God: for it is he that giveth thee power to get wealth, that he may establish his covenant which he sware unto thy fathers, as it is this day."

Proverbs 3:5-10, "Trust in the LORD with all thine heart; and lean not unto thine own understanding. In all thy ways acknowledge him, and he shall direct thy paths. Be not wise in thine own eyes: fear the LORD, and depart from evil. It shall be health to thy navel, and marrow to thy bones. Honour the LORD with thy substance, and with the firstfruits of all thine increase: So shall thy barns be filled with plenty, and thy presses shall burst out with new wine."

Matthew 6:33, "But seek ye first the kingdom of God, and his righteousness; and all these things shall be added unto you."

1 Chronicles 22:13, "Then shalt thou prosper, if thou takest heed to fulfil the statutes and judgments which the LORD charged Moses with concerning Israel: be strong, and of good courage; dread not, nor be dismayed."

Psalm 1:1-3, "Blessed is the man that walketh not in the counsel of the ungodly, nor standeth in the way of sinners, nor sitteth in the seat of the scornful. But his delight is in the law of the LORD; and in his law doth he meditate day and night. And he shall be like a tree planted by the rivers of water, that bringeth forth his fruit in his season; his leaf also shall not wither; and whatsoever he doeth shall prosper."

Job 36:11, "If they obey and serve him, they shall spend their days in prosperity, and their years in pleasures."